TIME IS GREATER THAN MONEY

VOLUME I

WRITTEN BY RAMÓN DE LA CRUZ

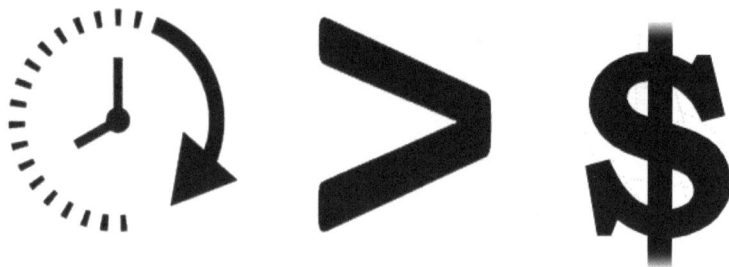

Time Is Greater Than Money
Volume 1

Ramon De La Cruz

<u>Upcoming works from 3DLCE books:</u>

(Available winter 2021- spring 2022 on : www.3DLCE.com)

- Time is greater than Money Vol.2 - the mixtape

- Time is greater than Money Vol. 2 (the lyrics) COMING SOON

- Mommy Loves/Daddy Loves – early reading for single parents and their children to introduce children to the person that is their parent.

- Mommy & Daddy Love, Daddy & Daddy Love, Mommy and Mommy Love - early reading for dual parents and their children to introduce children to the people that are their parents

Time Is Greater than Money:
Volume 1

Ramon De La Cruz

2021

First Printing: 2021

ISBN: 978-1-7371974-1-6

3DLCE LLC
723 Monroe Street #101
Rockville, MD 20850

3DLCE Publishing is accepting diversity submissions and collaboration. Contact us for more info via email at **shop@3DLCE.com**

Ordering Information:

Special discounts are available on quantity purchases by corporations, associations, educators, and others. For details, contact the publisher at the above listed address.

U.S. trade bookstores and wholesalers: Please contact us with your order by email at shop@3DLCE.com for Ramon De La Cruz or by telephone at (646) 548-7241

Dedication

Dedicated to Humankind…

with gratitude to the multiverse and its infinte power to deliver for us all.

Thank you.

Thank you.

Without the mentoring, wisdom and divine patience I found, I would have never achieved this dream – to share, inspire, motivate and most importantly to remind us to BE. I am grateful for the challenges, the opportunities and the blessings received and those yet to come.

Thank you.

"Yes: I am a dreamer.

For a dreamer is one who can only find his way by moonlight;

And his punishment is that he sees the dawn before the rest of the world."

— Oscar Wilde

Contents

Acknowledgements

Special thanks to my mother for building us with love, courage and laying within us the mysteries of the universe, through music. Thankful to have experienced love in beautiful forms and appreciate those lessons. Thankful for a lula.

Loving thanks to my children teachers, Jaden, Jonathan, Evan, Enzo, Mateo, Tomas and Christian. Thanks to my loving family, the best kind of support. Thanks to my mentors, professors, and to my best friends in the world Noe, Ant, Lips, Squirrel, Henny and G!

Love to all my boys and the Bronx because SON, we made it!
We are blessed. Go get yours. Let's collab when you're about your business.

I would also like to thank my teachers, my editor, my creative college classmates, and my cherished family without whose help this book would never have been completed.

Thank you for your patience and guidance. (mostly for your patience!)

Foreword

We are all born with Time. Few of us are born with Money. So this endeavor seeks to focus on a common denominator of our development: Our primary tool for task-mastering in the moment, Time. Time is the present. Time is the moment where we build *momentum* and can generate the energy we need to manifest our reality, however we see it. We have gated our spirits and our minds with fear and worry but, we can release and be open to the wonders this life has to offer. We can enjoy the balance. We can breathe easy while there is still work to do. We can enjoy the moment while focusing on the future, having learned from the past. We can (mentally) be in the three or four places at once – that's the benefit of existing in the 3rd dimension. So with the measure of life in mind, how we apply our time in the moment becomes the singular most effective resource for reaching our potential. I wrote this with hopes it inspires you to take YOUR time, invest in yourself and do what you love. Reach levels of greatness you never imagined then, recalculate your position and raise the bar. Neither greatness nor time are wasted and are always being invested but, what are we investing time into? Could our collective focus balance to value internal investments over monetary gain? Can we better appreciate the time we invest into making a life instead of the money we make in our lifetime? We need money for some things. Is the tradeoff of our time worth an "all eggs in one basket" type investment? Can we be that naïve in a "gig economy"? Can we be both aligned in purpose and profit? Can we do more? Can we be more? No. We are already more. Now, we take our time BEING more...one moment at a time.

Ramon De La Cruz
October, 2020

Preface

Connection is nirvana. We often seek peace outside when its energy is found within. Our energies are best focused internally, where we can affect change on the most important facet of our existence, ourselves. At times, we may feel ourselves lost, exhausted and overloaded. We are in unprecedented, historical times and it is in these times that we must turn inward and employ our most dominant resource to love ourselves, have patience and to propel ourselves upward. We spend a lot of time online, watching others live their lives, for some of us this generates happiness and, for others it generates fear. In the midst of this pioneering, dangerous yet, beautiful time it is most important that we learn how to balance and rebalance ourselves as this energy presents itself. That we are ready with love and able to guide one another, inspire and lift each other because we have prepared ourselves. "Time is greater than Money" started as an empowerment philosophy idea and evolved into something of a universal constant. A truth that says YOU MATTER and because you matter, your time (whose moments add up to become your life) matter as well. From pre-teenager to adulthood you are in control your time. I took my time to write this for you, to you and sometimes with you. I listened to many people, read and researched our human spirituality and meditated to see what truths would come to me and, what came to me was this: We can do this better. Life is not a rat-race, it's more of a monkey marathon (scientifically speaking). It's not a sprint, not a ¼ mile or a 40 yard dash. That may be how we attack the days and tasks we give ourselves but the long run, the BIG picture, the gran prix is slow. It accumulates with each thought, each feeling and each rise and fall. Remember, I am not saying that money does not matter. That's not realistic in the society we exist in at present. Money is a tool that some of us have. TIME is a tool that all of us have. It is our common thread and basis for self-love and even, how we may use money.

So let's spend some time together.

Time (noun)

...is the indefinite continued progress of existence and events that occur in an apparently irreversible succession from the past, through the present, into the future.

Money (noun)

...is something generally accepted as a medium of exchange, a measure of value, or a means of payment.

When did you first decide how much your time was worth?

Chapter 1: My Voice (Let Go)

Okay so, truth be told this was my first book title "Getting in touch with your inner dick". It was simply about getting around in a world that constantly tried to dictate who I was to me. After much research, discovering a woman wrote her version of that already and, study of group opinions were considered I grew. I realized my message was bigger than that. Albeit a part of a human's natural personal process of development, it's just that, one tool in the toolbox to be employed strategically. For whatever universal purpose, I had to develop that side to protect my empathic self from a challenging environment to grow up in. I also just wanted to use Dick to get your attention. It can be whoever...Barbara, Will, Jane, Jose, Abdoudjwe, whatever...whoever you are, that's your name and who need to get in touch with. I chose Dick because I needed to have a way to balance myself and protect my innocence from that abuse; having this concept helped me switch on toughness I needed. Growing up in New York City is a whole different timeline than most get to experience. I needed a way to get up, like we all do. From early on in life, I was very opinionated and self-confident, sometimes to a fault in others perceptions. Since childhood, my mom told me I could be and do anything I wanted so I ran with that. People later in life threw labels at me like gregarious (my HS principal wrote this in my recommendation letter), cocky, arrogant, and eventually, a 'dick' because I was unafraid in my delivery of my ideas and had the brash abandon of a teenager's communication style. I was told I was too strong a speaker for my age, too strong willed for my experience and didn't consider enough. I was told I didn't have enough experience. What they didn't see was a young man on his way to become an Eagle Scout despite being a boy enduring abuse at home due to domestic violence, bullying and street violence. What they did (and sometimes still do) see was every comfortable Latino stereotype to box me in to. The interesting thing I've learned about people's opinions is that they don't matter unless you let them. So I focused on myself. I learned and taught and paid attention from many life lessons, family, teachers, friends, mentors and masters. I thought I was well informed and was eager to share myself with others in hopes that they would share themselves with me, so we could both learn and grow from one another. I'm a hopeless romantic and reciprocity is one of my life's ideals. All I wanted to do was share what I had learned from my life and get some lessons in return, a fair trade I thought. All I got was grief about being a "dreamer" and for not doing enough to "fit in" from my teachers. This was such a contradictory thought for me to get my mind around. All the educational slogans like "Aim High" and "Be the best you can be" seemed like false advertisement in the real classroom. Sometimes, others lack of self-confidence won't allow them to see you, only your confidence and how it makes them feel. If they were confident and humble enough to see with the eyes of a child, we would not be perceived as a threat to their perception of self.   We would be another traveler with a perspective on the journey of our own to share. It is our responsibility to feel confident and comfortable with ourselves.

So if you have ever felt like your needs and wants were not being considered. If you've ever felt your kindness was taken advantage of or that your efforts went unreciprocated or un-appreciated. Yes, you - the other-oriented, "put others first" kind of person who thrives on making other people happy. You are caring, considerate and giving; always thinking about the needs of loved ones before your own – ignoring YOUR own in the process because we silently feel any kind of self-directed goodness is being selfish. I know you because I know myself…I was raised around great people like you, strong people, honest, good-natured and determined. Oftentimes, too selfless to be selfish but, don't our lives need a little of our own attention too? If Selfish and Selfless are the 2 opposite points on a line graph - the extremes - what is the middle ground considered? What's a healthy balance?

Self-love

Self-ish

Self-less

I think there we would find Self Love; a healthy, self-expression of appreciation, caring, nurturing, trust and communication. As the saying goes…"Don't we owe it to ourselves?" If we care, nurture, trust and communicate as individuals first, it will improve the whole human experience. We have to listen to and trust our intuition and bodies as they are divine instruments, no matter what your theory is about how we came to be. We have to care, nurture and love ourselves so we can define our expectations of love, and be able to share them with the right people in our lives. At times we feel our time, energy & efforts are unreciprocated and unappreciated; as if we give and, give and give with nothing (or not as much as we subconsciously expected) in return. As we've heard it so succinctly put - "They take and take and take and never give". Well, charity starts at home they say, so take care of your SELF first. Only when we are truly happy ourselves can we make another person or people happy. Why an Inner Dick? I went extreme with it to get your attention. It's really just your ID or identity. Get in touch with who you are and where you want to go, enjoy the journey, love yourself and good things will follow. Have faith. Faith is not something exclusive to religion. Faith starts within humanity and becomes religion so, believe in yourself first. The beauty within transforms the beauty we experience.

Then again, when you're too nice (to further illustrate my point of this transformation theory I present to you) Some of us need to develop an Inner Dick, (a Sasha Fierce to your Beyonce Knowles, so to speak or, a Spider Man to your Peter Parker); something to remind us to balance out our goodwill in a humorous yet, assertive kind of way that communicates and respects boundaries.

Your inner dick is your mental empowerment tool to remind you to do so without feeling guilty or selfish about it. You have the personal responsibility to take care of yourself, your dreams and life. You are supposed to be doing this. Get in touch with your ID. Survivors guilt (or survivors syndrome) is a real psychological hurdle for many of us who have experienced trauma in our life (everyone after 9/11/01)

Here are some case examples drawn from real experiences and observations:

"A" type gives their all to a job and career, defines themselves by what they do and not who they are. They have trouble trusting but treats the wrong people right and the right people wrong, possible creating a cycle of feelings of being betrayed constantly. They work extra hours, takes on all projects and doesn't feel compensated or appreciated. They often feels frustrated at work and with life in general.

My unprofessional opinion:
"A" has misplaced their trust, thus creating unrealistic expectations of others.

My unprofessional suggestion:
"A" needs to take responsibility for their own happiness.

"B" type is a highly educated, strong and, independent person who is manipulated by their family. Their family may use guilt for being successful and abuse with requests for money. B allows their kindness to be taken advantage of due to a sense of duty because nothing is ever enough for their family.

My unprofessional opinion:

"B "may be misdirecting their generosity and charity. Being selfless to an extreme can be too generous, especially if one is not in a position to assist. Abusive relationships for both men and women are really about over-caring for people who don't have your best interests in mind.

My unprofessional suggestion:

Consider investing energy/emotion similar to the way you learn to balance your financial investments

"C" type are the Elderly, our parents, caregivers or grandparents who can't say no to their kids on helping family with things like babysitting their grandkids, borrowing money, feel bad saying no even though it inconveniences them sometimes. Retired and having to raise children again due to irresponsible parents, un-attentive parents or just career parents.

My unprofessional opinion:

"C" type may be unable to say no or feel guilty if they disappoint someone else, or can't help

My unprofessional suggestion:

There's a code for rescuers, a saying we have in teamwork situations and that's that if you are in trouble and need help, in my rescue effort I have to make sure to avoid the same perils that you fell prey. If not, we run the risk of increasing the number of people in danger who need help. In life we should follow the same code

The purpose of this journey through yourself is to learn about your Self; how to appreciate yourself and how to find a way to express that self-love in a healthy way. The way we love ourselves; the way we treat and view ourselves, is what we will subconsciously impart onto and, expect of others. So to make this world a better place, we have to make ourselves better people; making the place we are all in better. If each of us can reach our individual potential points, then we as a people will transcend our perceptions of existence and create a whole new way of life.

> ## "Don't wish for peace. Manifest peace in your SELF; Then share it with the world. Bring your peace to the table"
> ### Ramon De La Cruz

I believe in the extraordinary potential in each of us. The only way to help the human race evolve is for each of us to accept the divine responsibility of ourselves. Only then can we truly help one another. Whatever you believe, whatever your religion or spiritual beliefs are, we can all agree on universal truths like: Love, Peace and Happiness. They can't be achieved without a concerted effort. So, instead of expending that energy externally, (by obsessing about other people's lives or material items), invest it internally on your Self and on those who truly deserve the blessing that is your presence, energy and being.

Once you've fulfilled YOUR goals to your expectations, then move on to other areas of happiness like Family and Friends.

Your Inner Dick is your self-empowerment model to a better, happier you. A NEW Bold, Unconventional, Adaptable and Determined you. Determination comes from Confidence; Confidence from familiarity with good Planning; Good Planning from Research; Research comes from exploring what you Love. That a reverse engineering of Self. Love is a verb, not a noun. You have to choose to Love, you have to have self-awareness to know what to love and also self-love to be disciplined enough to go with what will work for you. Pure Love with no objective judgment is reckless. Reserve purely emotional love for certain special moments; Use your judgment wisely when it comes to matters of the heart. Allow people to prove themselves, before you give totally of yourself.

It's the choice that some of us make by not making. We choose NOT to follow our hearts, our dreams and instead choose for something more secure like a 9-5 job. What is security but a dream? How is it that we find security in someone else's dreams but not our own? This is essentially what we do when we take a job working for someone else, instead of creating a job of our own. In each company that I have ever worked for, I found a way to rise to the top and be promoted. I found that my skills, talents and expertise matched or outweighed that of the people supervising me. So why put my skills to work for someone else when I could just as easily, and with a lot more enjoyment, redirect that effort to make myself financially stable and independent? I could, whenever I chose to.

When at any moment our lives can be snatched, how can we be so naïve and believe in something as dreamful as security provided by another? There is no security, you can be sure of that. There is no magic wand that turns all the years we spend on work into life. Spend your life on YOUR life. Spend your time, on your dreams. Decide what you mark you will make, where your impact will be felt and what legacy you will leave. Then, begin your journey. You can have all the happiness you want, all the money you want, all the material items you want. All we must do is choose to seek it. Ask and ye shall receive. Ask through meditation, prayer, conversation, journal entry, email to god or however you choose. The point of it all is not what we choose but that we choose something. We choose to lay the responsibility of our lives on Destiny, God or Circumstance but, it is all up to us. That responsibility (Response-ability) to self is heavy. We silently think its ok to put ourselves to the side for work, love, sometimes kids and family. It is up to us and will be up to us about 95% of the time. We choose that so, why not choose something better for ourselves? Get in touch with your Inner Dick.

My unprofessional suggestion:

Be a dick with yourself first. Discipline is the first form of self-love. It makes us forsake the present pleasure for a future reward. With things like work projects, fitness and nutrition be disciplined. Form a comfortable routine, create your reality as you wish it to be. Start with the hardest things first and, it's all downhill from there. Be disciplined with yourself, be a Dick sometime with others and don't let yourself be complacent or lazy. It makes most sense to go for whatever you want with gusto; to chase the hardest parts first so the rest will be easier. I created this method whenever I had homework or a project to complete. It mentally helped me ease up, relax and allow things to come to me.

Introduction to your Inner Dick
We all have one - Here's how you get in touch with it.

Firstly, it is A-OK to get in touch with your Inner Dick. Your Inner Dick is a combination of things. It is your inner self, the purest concentrated form of you; your essence or your spirit. Dick is the part of you that lives bravely and fully; confidently and aware. Dick is your intuition, until you give him the stage to be more. Dick is your conscience, your voice of reason or your "id" of clarity. Dick is your being in the right place at the right time guide. Life teaches us to quiet DICK down, that we should crawl back under the rock we came from and accept life as it is. Dick teaches us to write LIFE as we wish it to be, to be brave enough to follow your dreams and to bring your opinions to the table. Getting in touch with your Inner Dick is not about being an asshole. It's about being the person you were intended to be, contributing your part to the human experience.

You are a person underneath all that life you've heaped upon yourself...Strip away all the layers of conditioning and clothes and, deep down, there you are. Someone who isn't listened to, loved, or cared for enough? Could it be because we don't love or care enough about ourselves? Could it be we don't listen to ourselves enough? Is it that life matches our efforts the way Fortune 500 companies match 401k plans? Is this what we could be missing?

It is becoming more and more apparent in our experiences that humans rely on one other too much, that they aren't being actively self-aware and don't self-serve enough. Some of us have gotten lazy, complacent and content in letting life pass us by like it's meaningless. We are overly dependent on each other and are disconnected from the very things which make us feel alive. We can see the evidence in our economic crisis and in our local communities. We have traded our divine status as CREATORS for the more comfortable and "less stressful" CONSUMERS. Being a consumer isn't really less stressful though, is it?

The world we all live in is designed to do one thing. Get our Money & Time. Take our Money. Give us less Money for our Time. Charge us for the Time it takes to pay back the Money. It's exhausting and probably the biggest investment of our energy is exerted on the mental aspect of it. When I go shopping I know what I want and want to find it, buy it and leave as fast as possible. Some of us exhaust ourselves physically, emotionally and mentally; and this constant flow of diversions and information is designed so to keep us feeling overwhelmed, so we are constantly dependent. In order to improve our lives personally, we should plan to get out of this system of income to debt. Only way for that is to invest your money. Take small risks ($1,500-5,000), diversify your interests and pay attention to your money. Save your money. Set months where there is a no buy zone in effect. Saving takes diligence and discipline, two things that are hard to come by when you want something. Use your strength to be strong. Be independent. Set your own trends. Be your SELF.

For example: There is a divide of effort which leads to some needing the assistance of others. It is diminishing the magic of America, the Middle Class. A down Economy, High Unemployment and Social Services resources are being used faster than the funds that sustain them can be replenished. We as a people, Humanity, are overspending financially and Spiritually. We are putting more out there than we can handle, over-extending ourselves, our monies and, our bodies.

LESS = MORE.

It's time to redirect our focus and energies; To reaffirm our own individual existences with personal investments and, to experience the aural expansion that awaits us. Simply put, if we invested less of ourselves into unsuccessful ventures and relationships, then, we could re-invest that into ventures and relationships which are fruitful and fulfilling to us. When we give ourselves the freedom and respect we deserve, life will respond.

Observe and Redirect:
- Observe the areas in your life where you are over investing your energy. Job, Love Interest, Diet, Vices etc.
- Redirect the time you spend in those areas to areas that return for you.

To write this book, I used 15-45 minutes lunch breaks, 3 days a week; Redirecting my focus and energy from making money for others at my job - to investing my time and MONEY to create something meaningful and fulfilling for ME.

In the same way you would invest more money in a gaining account to earn more dividends, you invest more time in yourself to get more back. Knowledge is power. The more knowledge you have, as cliché as this sounds, the more powerful you feel. I was advanced placements classes all through school and got a college education before I graduated High School. Once I learned school's purpose, to teach us how to teach ourselves and others, my path became clear. School prepares you to create in life. Which is why so many of us feel lost after going through 4-8 years of Higher education, only to end up managing someone else's cash cow.

We are all brave souls. My purpose here is to share my experiences and inspire you. I'm self-taught and feel so much more satisfied for it. I've been inspired by life and I can relate to people who stood for something and made it work by any means necessary. Whether you are religious or not, there is no doubt in my mind that we were fashioned in the image of the creator because of how FREE we ALL feel, when we are creating. It is a shared emotion, look how we "relate" to freeing concepts like being financially independent, saying what you want-however you want to say it and creating new worlds in cyberspace. Creation is the key to the happiness of the human race.

If we were all focused on creating a better world for ourselves, we'd create a better world for each other as a by-product of our efforts.

As selfish and sad as this may sound, it is not your responsibility to be submissive or change how you speak or behave around others because they are not comfortable with what you are. On the contrary, we want to consider the effect our delivery has on others and use it strategically. Develop the voice, that's the journey to sharing our narratives. It is ok to say "I am comfortable with what I am and that is what I am here to share." Your situation, that's a "Y.S." - Your situation. This is an important step for your Inner Dick: having the courage to hold each person accountable for happiness in their own existence. More in theme with the larger message of time being greater than money, it is being accountable for your own happiness.

Be able to put the onus back on others for their own lives.

That's how you free up the time you need to invest on yourself; by doing less for others that can do it for themselves. (Obviously, children and the disabled/elderly are exempt from this but, what we do for them is a labor of love – but even these cases can be applied at times.) It feels scary to let go but it is the only way to grow.

Let go of your fear of the unknown. You know what's known about the un-known? That it's always going to be there. Be brave, be well prepared and have faith in your efforts. Everything will work out in the best way for you if you take the right steps. There is no "karmic recession" and there never will be...All the en-ergy we need is there for each and every one of us. Ask and ye shall receive...

My mom was always a driver for me in following my dreams. She didn't let life deny her the chance to follow hers and I have always admired her for that. All my life, I was told to be different, stand out, trust yourself and display your talents. In everyday life though, this is not what is needed, so I chose to remove myself from the cycle that is everyday life. I hope my energies in these works I created for you with love in my heart and mind, inspire you to do the same.

Lifetimes are small so do things
BIG

Let go..

Your effort towards your development will be the catalyst to the progression of your life. Getting in touch with your Inner Dick is about being focused in your efforts to grow your SELF. That is the essence of your inner dick – not so much to be a dick but, to be kind and disciplined enough with your energy and time so as to give freely without worry on returns, because you provide returns to yourself. Be disciplined with yourself. Remember to see Life as it truly is; Raw, Live and uncensored. Maintain your vision but don't fool yourself into thinking you've succeeded. Remember to see life as it really is. When reality matches your vision and you are reaping the benefits of your efforts then make sure you celebrate. It's important to celebrate our victories. Sometimes, it's what makes the toil worthwhile because it means spending time with the people we love.

Don't lose hope of finding your path or perfect match. For each one of us beautiful humans there is someone of comparable polarity out there to complement us and help us on our journey. For each one of us there is a comfortable and distinct path that calls us. It's ok and even necessary for our wellbeing to make people important to us happy. It ties into our essential need for companionship.

However, it is not ok if the energy and effort is not reciprocated. That's physically equivalent to continually running in to a brick wall; draining, ineffective, very painful and, counter-productive to your efforts. To get ahead, we need to stop running into the brick wall, assess the situation and find a new path to reach our destination; same thing with emotional control, which is a by-product of mastering your SELF. (Not that there's anything wrong with making people happy - we all should, on an appropriate scale, try to improve each other's conditions- just not when it's at the expense of our reach or wellbeing. ("Reach or wellbeing" = our financial range or our physical capacity.)

For years this was part of who I was as a young entertainer in New York City. I lived for the audience's interactions, for standing ovations and for the raw emotion and associated high of live performances. The energy you feel could make you addicted. We were performing twice a week, first at Charity and School events, then Yankee Stadium and Madison Square Garden. It was fun and singing is my deepest passion so I literally lived my dreams out and loved every minute of it.

The group I thought of as brothers, that I put my heart and soul into and put together won a contest and were flown to San Diego, CA. to perform at the MTV Beach House. We came in 3rd in a nationally televised battle of the bands and were tested on what I thought was going to be a trip to put us on the map. To my surprise, when we landed back in NY the group disbanded. It came to be that some of the other members in the group had different agendas than I did. It saddened me and was a turning point in my life. I reached a point where I would put music on the back burner and focus on a career.

I wanted different things, in the sense that we all grow up and want more meaningful things to go with our material things. Time passes and we realize the accumulation of wealth is the smaller part of the equation: The accumulation of LIFE, and the moments that make it up, are the greater part of the equation. The material items are layered and complemented with pets, a spouse and children sometimes. For me, it was time for a re-evaluation of my life. I was living a fast life of easy (legal) money, beautiful women and 36 hour days. Burning the candle at both ends and I had was some great memories to show for it. Nothing wrong with that of course but, it came to me that I could accept great memories or I can make my memories greater. Sounds strange right? I'll admit that much but, I was a family guy at heart. I grew up with a large family, 2 brothers, a sister and a thousand cousins. Some were just married and it was in our birth order it would seem to be my turn to take the plunge and have a family of my own. So I slowed myself down enough to ask some questions…

"What am I doing?
How does this benefit me?
Where do I want to be?
What do I need to get there?
Should I dream and do or maintain and accept?"

It's great to follow a dream, but, if it's not paying the bills, life keeps moving is how I saw it. To some of us that would mean quit but, for me it meant try harder. Days passed, bills piled up and dreams had to give way to income producing positions to maintain the chase of my dream. I couldn't give up on my passion for music totally but had to redirect it and focus it in certain time slots. After work, I began recording at a studio near my job. That developed into me investing into a studio of my own and starting my company 3DLCE LLC. I thought of my job as fund raising so I could do what I loved with the goal being to turn a profit from the sales of the original material I produced. I didn't need a lot of sales either, since all my music was original, my investment my own with little debt and, I will make and keep most of my profits. I have to maintain a job with benefits for my life's day-to-day responsibilities but, I never lost touch of who I was and stayed true to my Self. My point is, what we really need is to be able to produce income from a source that not only provides us with financial means but, personal fulfillment as well.

For most of us, a 9-5 job fits the bill for this need, but only temporarily. Time passes and the convenience of the 9-5 job leads to years and eventually some retire from a job they thought was only temporary. The houses and material things they wanted are on the backseat now. Somehow, whatever dreams or goals they had ends up with them. We negotiate the surrender of ourselves by deferring LIFE. LIFE is NOW, happening all the time, Right NOW. Now for many of us means after normal work hours or "the 5 to 9", as they call it. Waiting for it puts the onus on someone else. Go get it.

To "wait" to live your LIFE "after" you retire and are eligible for your pension, is an outright lie. Jobs that tell us this are LIES. We cannot stop LIFE by simply not living. Life keeps on going. We make that choice to defer life but, it does not join us. We make a conscious decision to stop living and all it takes is a little stern discipline to reverse our decision. LIFE, when we give up on our dreams, isn't life, it is ROUTINE. Robotic, Atrocious and Blasphemous in the way it wastes our most precious resource – LIFE/TIME. LIFE begins to live us and we call this surviving. If we were in an ocean, you would be happily treading water when you could swim to shore.

Most of us hopelessly look out at the immense expanse of the sea instead of looking in the direction of something closer and more attainable, even if it's a small island. (And for anyone who has ran or started businesses, in the beginning, all there is, is a small island).

Living life is done most effectively by bringing your ideas to fruition, planning their completion, setting goals and meeting your goals. Life is simple in this regard. Just Do IT! Get out there and live it, make your mistakes, learn your lessons and be better than anyone thought you could be. Then be the best you can be...or survive day to day, check to check, rite of passage to rite of passage hoping blindly that life will somehow improve itself if we can just survive a little longer...If we could work the next Su-Su, or if we can hit the number or just make that dollar into a dream with that lotto game. I'd rather invest my dollar while I am awake while some of those kinds of dreamers keep sleeping... invest in the future of ideas. Take some manageable risks and try something new. Anything less is simple survival.

Is surviving really *living*?

What about our true purpose for being? Each of us is drawn in a certain direction – we all feel it. The divining rods within us all, drawing us to our natural path is always at work. Even when we don't want it to, somehow we find our way back where we are supposed to be. We must be aware of what this is for ourselves, nurture it, develop it and, learn to do what makes us feel good. It is a brave first step into this new paradigm of being but one that ultimately will benefit us all in the long term, allowing us to focus on more important things facing our species.

Getting in touch with your inner dick means getting rid of the fear of success, of the guilt Society and Religion has conditioned us to feel if something feels good. Here's a divine secret - IT'S ALL GOOD, in moderation; anything can be bad in excess. Even religion as most wars have been fought in the name of god. It's a universal concept but, I believe in the good in all of us and our innate ability to know what is right, true and just. We ALL have the potential, now all we need is the push that can only come from within. Everyone needs a little excitement in life, but only we can give it to ourselves. Only we truly know what we need.

Life has a way of taking us where we set the auto-pilot to. We get caught up in the flow of a routine - of a career or a family - and don't realize this is our choice. This is the way we choose to use our time. Time seems to slip away faster as more precious things are added. We begin to feel overwhelmed and stressed due to the natural pressures and the responsibilities of life and living it; so much so that we are content to allow it to live us. We give up, in a way, on life, simply because we choose to stop living it. We choose…

My mom always had quotes around the house when we were growing up. The one that stuck with me most was, "When you're through improving yourself, you're through!" When we stop challenging ourselves and settle for maintaining who we are, instead of striving for who we want to be, we stop our own development. Operate out of your comfort zone, because your comfort zone is a false sense of security we've created. The reality of Life is that it can be taken from us at any moment and eventually, we all will have our moment. That alone should be enough motivation to inspire us to live our lives in honor of the blessing that Life is.

Although it may seem impossible or so overwhelmingly immense that we may never get there, we must always have ideals – our highest goals to achieve in LIFE–

and what better goal to have then to bring our ideal of LIFE into Reality.   Life is what we make it – like the song says.   We are each naturally responsible for our own happiness, well-being and mental health.   This is an integral part of getting in touch with your inner dick.   Once you master this part, you can expect this of other people and, this will increase the quality of your relationships.

There is a natural energy that exists between us and we are each Captains of maintaining our respective energies, including happiness.   When we assume some- one else's pursuit of happiness, we are thieves in the flow of life, slowing the natural path of development.   We are caught between being good people, thinking we are helping a person when we are actually making them more dependent.   Two sayings come to mind:

> "Give a man a fish and he will eat for a day.
> Teach a man to fish and he will eat every day."

Because we're not in touch with our Inner Dicks - because we feel guilty or just can't say, no – we actually say yes to things that dampen the flow of energy be- tween us.   The energy between us is LIFE.   Letting go is so much more liberating.

> *(Now, there are exceptions to every rule of course–*
> *when we're helping a friend or a cause,*
> *or someone loved and respected or in dire need –*
> *These are the few exceptions to the rule.*
> *We are thieves in the flow of life when we assume*
> *someone else's pursuit of happiness.*
> *Each person has a responsibility to self,*
> *to their own evolution and happiness.*
> *We each have a responsibility to each other*
> *to allow each other the space and time for that journey.)*

We are a beautiful, loving, brave and strong people.   Let's expect that of one another.   Have faith in each other because we will survive anything life throws at us together.   Our minds will grow and our horizons will expand in due time.   We are each on our own road of development: of self- awareness, discipline, self-esteem building, dream attainment and mastery.   Patience is a virtue because it shows grace and humility.   So wave at a fellow dream seeker when you pass; treat them the way you would want to be treated.   Help them out and you will have karma on your side.

Life is good and getting better. In my mind, **I was being brave enough to be myself**, being content and, proud of myself enough to share my thoughts and emotions…my many opinions and be a free independent thinker – question authority when needed and be a creator, inventor and bring something to this world and, ultimately, be vulnerable and open to the worlds emotions, perceptions and vision. But to people who weren't as outspoken or extroverted or didn't share my exuberance on life, I was careless and selfish because I wasn't taking their feelings into consideration. I felt like it wasn't my responsibility to take their feelings into consideration, not because I didn't care but because it is their responsibility to express themselves. How was I to take a feeling into consideration that I wasn't aware of? So I got to thinking about how to empower people, anyone and everyone, to be strong enough to say what they want, be who they want and do what they want? So I'm Dick, by destiny not by choice…what's your name? … It's nice to meet you ☺

Know thy I.D. & Love thy I.D.

You don't have to be a Dick, you just have to not be afraid to be yourself, even if it offends some people initially. This is our self's way of weeding out the undesirable influences in our life, people you may need a break from, by making us feel uncomfortable around them. You don't have to be a DICK to everyone, just assert yourself so people can know the real you.

It is who we are now that determines who we will be in the future. By controlling the now, we can change the future. Who do you want to be? Knowing who you are is very important. If History repeats itself, knowing our personal histories is vital to reaching wherever we want to go. What was will be or, History is the story of what was and what will be. Our lives all have cycles. If we are self aware and can be objective in judging our self (which is what scientists say separates us from animals) in order to improve ourselves we break the cycles and start new, more productive and beneficial cycles.

The Greeks, well actually, the Egyptians said "Know thy Self" and they have proven to be timeless reminders of the need to be self-aware. This is the first step to change. Give yourself some time. When were you born? Where were you born, under what circumstances? What was your childhood like? Where did you naturally gravitate in life; what are your life's common denominators? What are your school year memories? How did you get where you are today? Once you've answered the questions try mental projection. Think of where you want to go, focusing on the details of the plan as you go and the end result you desire. It is within us to achieve the heights we set for ourselves. The question is not who we are but, who will we be? Always thinking ahead and planning ahead is what affords us the mental clarity to truly enjoy the present, worry-free.

Q - It's been a long time. How do I get to know myself?

A - Well, here are some exercises:

1 - Keep a journal, Write daily and read it in three months. This will help you see your life objectively.

2 - Go on a date (movies, dinner, shopping) with **yourself.**

Treat yourself like you would treat a potential love interest, kindly and attentively.

3- Take time DAILY for yourself to focus your mind, to relax and meditate, and to feel your inner peace.   15-30 minutes and on days you have less time meditate for 30-60 minutes.

4- Seek Change and be the change you seek. If you see something you can improve, do something about it. Walk your talk.

THOUGHT: We are all self-contained universes. Productive habits and Counter-Productive habits ripple out into the many worlds within us. The better one of us becomes, the better we all become.

NOTE: Human bodies fully regenerate every 7 years - Meaning every cell in our body changes every 7 years. At ages 7, 14 21, 28, 35, etc, get ready to meet the new you! Look at your pictures, how do your 7 year periods look?

-The great Burden & Freedom of our responsibility to Self.

"With great power comes great responsibility" – Stan lee

If knowledge is power, then once you know something the onus, the POWER is given to you to do something with. Use the power. Now that you know yourself, it's on you to use that what you've learned to improve your environment and your life. This "something" is for each one of us to decide, once we are in tune with that knowledge/power-responsibility that comes through self-awareness. Responsibility is your "response-ability", your method of responding to something within your abilities. Plan your work, work your plan. You can do it. It's just up to you what you do. You are what you choose and the outcomes of our choices help us form perceptions. We create good and bad, in accordance to an events relation to our life. Perception then becomes reality after we believe it long enough. We condition ourselves to believe it and we strive to maintain a good perception amongst our peers and loved ones – to reaffirm our own perceptions, maintain their acceptance and respect. All this just to give us a (false) sense of control over our life when all we can do is perceive our environment and the reactions of those among us- then turn that into this tale called reality. This perception is our clay to mold in the fabric of time. So how we think of things, is how they are.

This is the true power of the mind. Good thoughts lead to good returns. Everything you put out into the world through thought or word, comes back like a boomerang. So to control your world, first control your thoughts. What you put in is what you get out, just like our school or our bodies. Put in only good productive thoughts and practice this through meditation until its second nature. A good book to read is "As a Man Thinketh" by James Allen. We are physically limited by what our minds can perceive. What we perceive and believe we can achieve.

THOUGHT: We are all on the same road, to the same place. Life leads ultimately to a transformation we call Death, but it is not truly so. While it is a change in our physical state, the time we have here together is a chance to make things better. Every moment and every morning we are blessed with is another chance to bring good into the world. Try to make something better for someone. It could be a random act of kindness, it could be a planned act of positivity or, a good thought for someone you know and love. The point is to put something positive out there and you will get back something positive - If not for the good of all then for the most selfish reason of all, for you to benefit when it comes back around. We cannot escape our destinies, the same way the Earth can't escape its orbit around the Sun. We, as planets, revolve around our various stars in life, our careers, jobs and associations. This is our path, our link to destiny. We are on this path, that's our Destiny. How we walk this path, this determines our Fate. Physicists say time flows in an everlasting figure eight. What has been will be and that History repeats itself.

The questions are... What will you learn from History? What History will you write and, What History will be written of you? You must first know where you are from to know where you are going. Getting in touch with your Inner Dick is not about being negative. It's about knowing yourself, being confident and having faith in the flow. Being yourself without guilt; being a little charitable and a little selfish; Being in control of your life and enjoying it to the fullest.

You must understand yourself, your needs, your wants and how to motivate yourself. Some people are Leaders, Some are followers. Life is like a Monet, we start up close to the picture seeing only a color and as we grow older, we step back and begin to see more of our life's picture. Some people need to go to College,

Some people need tests, some people need to learn through life. We each need to learn how we best learn. This is the purpose of school, to teach us first how to learn, then specific subjects and lastly how to teach. We need to know ourselves and all the intricacies that make us who we are. Start small, figure yourself out first. Take the time, take the test or follow your dream – whatever. Just decide to do something, make a plan and do it.

Know yourself, Test yourself, see what you're made of. Challenge yourself physically, mentally. Try something new, out of your comfort zone. Accept the results with love and move forward with the knowledge to change. It's important we love ourselves, speak lovingly in our thoughts and accept things. This is ultimately how we will treat others. We want the best out of others so we give the best of ourselves.

THOUGHT: Think about what I enjoy… What I seek in life, Where I am and What decisions brought me here, what benefits me most, what do I love doing and what are my talents? Once you get the picture, love yourself, accept yourself and have patience with your development. Care for yourself physically, mentally, spiritually and emotionally.

Physically – Exercise, Meditation, Nutrition, Companionship

Spiritual – Faith, Meditation

Emotional – Inner Dialogue, Relationships

Mental – Quiet, Peace, Rest

We are who we have made ourselves. The decisions we make during life have brought us here.

So to make the future what we seek, we must first make the moment what we seek.

Break it down to its simplest structure.

Our future is made of these moments…these moments in Time.

Time is what we must master next. Hence the choice…"To be or not to be"

Time investment & life simplification for facilitation of happiness

It has been said that time is money. I think that's wrong. Time is priceless and the price of money clearly fluctuates. Hence Time is worth more than money. In my opinion money doesn't even come close. This is an important perspective to keep in mind when we take jobs. We need to ask ourselves, "How much is my time, my LIFE, worth?" Remember how much you settle for when you take your next job. Think highly of your Self no matter who you are. The reality is that we need Time to make money so we can better enjoy our Time here. This is the cycle. Money cannot generate time and If anything is true about money, is it usually is put to good use for our fun – but Time flies when you're having fun. So money actually makes Time pass faster? Money is limitless while Time is limited. Money can be lost, you can lose $20 bucks and make it up somehow, but you can't lose 20 minutes and make them up. They're gone forever therefore they're priceless and non-renewable. Richard says - Expect more for your time. DICK SAYS...DEMAND more for your time. But balance this demand out and Give more than is expected. Step by step, plan your work and work your plan, the journey of 1,000 miles begins with one step. If you fail to plan, you plan to fail. Respect your time by investing it wisely and expect the same in return.

Don't say it. Just DO it.

Life is simple, we achieve by planning and doing. Sometime we get in our own way – wrapped in thought and wonder instead of focused on action and result. Do MORE doing and less complaining about what others are or are not doing. When this happens, you initiate a chain reaction between your mind and your life. You connect the two. You can't ask of someone something you are not willing to do yourself. Build good energy and karma by doing more and talking less. That's really the essence of this, to be in tune with self. Did you know that there is a frequency we all vibrate at, a harmonic with which we are all in tune. Look it up. I can't tell you everything. (F#). We are born with two ears and one mouth, the saying goes, to listen more than we speak. Listen, Plan and Do. Your word is your reputation so use it wisely. Your words are power and, when combined with the visualizing powers of the mind, can make miracles. Watch what you wish for and Use your power wisely. Honor your epiphanies when they come to you.

-Self Mastery-

The first part of this was to *know thy self*. *Mastering your self* comes from applying what you've learned to make progress towards your goals; personally evolving thru Self-Accountability, good judgment and awareness of your continuing development. Mastery is reaching a level of personal Excellence. Never Settle for Mediocrity when excellence is possible. Teach yourself; learn to learn from life's lessons. School's intent is to teach us how to read between the lines of life to absorb the lessons on our own. Once we've learned this, schools purpose if purely societal and/or perception/goal driven. Keep yourself in tune, on top of current events and local news. Know thyself means to know your surroundings, environment and world. Keep reading books, novels and keep growing your mind. We have to keep learning and relearning because as fast as we can adapt to new things they evolve.

-Meditation&Focus-

This is a topic I've talked about frequently with people all throughout my life. Meditation or, The Art of Breath as I like to call it is so obvious we look past it more often than not. Think of this for a second, we are born into this world and the Doctor spanks us to get us to take a breath. The next time we are taught about breath is when we run out of it, usually learning to swim, or run, or play an instrument and sing. I've had the benefit of all the varied disciplines and believe this is an important point of development for the human mind and body. In order to truly focus ourselves, we have to consciously develop our 4 points: Physical, Emotional, Mental and Spiritual with Exercise, Relationships, Education and Meditation, respectively. Physics says we are all energy, vibrating at different speeds. I believe breath is the key to opening and focusing the human mind and uniting it with the spiritual energy. We have 3 levels of the mind, Sub-conscious, Conscious and Super-Conscious. The smartest man, Albert Einstein, when measuring his brain activity only registered 10% usage. Imagine going through life using only one finger your whole life... A mind is a wonderful muscle to work, our strongest in fact. Work out your minds. Paint your own Picasso, you are the artist of your life. Master your own Monet. Collect your consciousness and unite it with the collective consciousness. I meditate to achieve this. I see it as experiential uploading into the collective conscious. So to master your own monet, you have to be able to have a "Monet Moment", time to see both the moment and future simultaneously. Think about it like this, you are looking at an impressionist painting or one who uses dots of paint to create larger images – you can focus on the beauty or randomness of each dot and you can both enjoy what the collective dot formation creates. In life, we can apply that to how we react in time and, self-control comes with breath control. Human physiological reaction to stress is to hold our breath.

So take one...and release it.

MEDITATION TECHNIQUES

THOUGHT: It's crazy to think that I have been meditating since I was 15 years old. I was a different child than my peers. I enjoyed my time alone to think. I was raised by a single parent; my dad was around sometimes. Despite that, I never felt lonely. I never felt alone. Maybe that's a by-product of growing up in NYC, where it seemed at times that there were more people per square mile than China. I was reassured by the fact that every time I thought I had an original thought, someone else would have it. Be it an invention idea, a song lyric or melody, a book concept - I gleaned that no one has proprietary rights to knowledge.

It is universal, it is communal, and it is accessible by all who seek it.

I remember when my mom found me laying on the floor in the living room she said (with a hint of panic) "Ramon, are you ok?" It roused me from my meditation with a startled giggle. It was the longest I've meditated for, 6-7 hours that felt like 1-2 hours at most. Once your mind is quiet and at peace, even time disappears. The veils of the mind are lifted through physical focus, science of breath and active peace. Hey, that sounded so good it's going in my book I said.

And it did.

Honor your epiphanies. Take notes faithfully because you never know when something will work.

The First rule of mental mastery is to calm your mind, to focus your mind.

Bring yourself into a physical place of peace to gather your SELF –

Nothing else, no music (yet),

                              no distractions.

Disconnect yourself from the Matrix, no TV, phone or Computer on.

No lights on either.

The best time to meditate is just before dawn, somehow the energy is strongest then. Something about the natural light coalescing with your aura, the natural energy we all emanate. I don't pretend to know everything, I'm just a keen observer. You may be that too. To do this we need to calm that need to observe, rather, we need to turn that energy inward.

To bring your mind to a state of peace, your surroundings need to put your physical self at peace. Every detail matters when you are trying to center yourself. A clean & quiet room, the library, outside with Nature, wherever, the point is to have solitude. Allow yourself to experience the natural comfort of being alone. The closest we usually come to this every day is while bathing. The bathroom becomes an escape, a moment of privacy to collect your Self. Find a new place that you use just to meditate just to be alone to visualize yourself in positive places with a clear mind. I use this time in my recording room to read & write, to listen to music or to focus on my plans and goals. Once you get your mind focused properly, your body follows. It's not a fast or slow process. It is as long as it takes for each of us. This soothing nature of the bathing experience is reminiscent of being in the womb as a child. It helps release endorphins that help us feel happy, relaxed and calm. It is in this calm where our most important self-direction happens. The silence helps you to hear your thoughts and only your thoughts. It brings your mind to a calm point.

You are here.

Next, we focus on the first thing we do when were born, breathe. And that's the last time we think about it. Isn't it reasonable that such an important part of our existence should be mastered beyond natural reflex?

Concentrate on controlling and focusing your breath and mind.

Inhale deeply through your nose and mouth then exhale fully until you empty your lungs.

Repeat three times.

Visualize an empty writing board on the wall. It's clean, shiny, brand new and, waiting for your first thoughts.

Most importantly, your slate is clean. This is your visualization tool for clearing your mind. We literally have to "see it clear".

While breathing, keep your mind's eye focused throughout the meditation –

Focus all your energy on your thoughts. Remember the details you create.

Visualize yourself traveling to a staircase (what kind of staircase?), reaching a door (what kind of door) and seeing a lock, finding a key and inserting it into the lock, turning the key and opening the lock, focus on the details – the sound the lock makes when turned and opened, what kind of lock it is, etc.)

Open the door, there is a staircase leading down. You descend each step, counting down slowly from 100 to 1. Mentally take each step.

Once reaching the bottom, you reach a passageway, a tunnel, a portal, another door or, whatever you envision. Go through and you are where? You are wherever makes you feel at peace and serene. Imagine a place where you feel safe, secure, at peace and loved, except now we learn to feel that way even when we are alone. A by-product of this exercise if that we can wean ourselves off of the dependency to companionship and learn to enjoy them freely again. This is the place for you to dream your dream, see the dream happening step by step. See yourself in a successful position as a result of your good work. See yourself relaxed in the world you create. Feel relaxed. This is the reason we go from controlling our breathing back to autopilot. It tells the body who's the boss and gives us the perspective of being in control of our selves, of our most basic function. This is your training space for mastering your mind. This is where extra-sensory abilities and mental expansion are possible. This is where we can tap into our super-conscious.

Where you go from here is up to you.

To complete our meditative journey, I like to end with gratitude for the universal forces that allow me to be, to live and that continually bless me beyond my understanding. I imagine myself bathed in light, glowing as if being charged from an in infinite source and charging my aura to protect me, my loved ones, friends, future, ancestors and the world. We end by crossing our arms and bowing our heads in humility to the great unknown saying, Thank you, Thank you, Thank you. The power is in what we believe. So, can you believe in yourself?

Sleep Meditation –

ROYGBV, red, orange, yellow, green, blue & violet

Take 3 deep breaths in and out, repeat three (3x) times

Clear your mind and visualize the colors of the rainbow slowly coming at you or surrounding you. Keep your eyes closed and focus on seeing the colors. Use things you can see clearly in your mind from nature like grass, the sky, clouds at dusk, the sun, etc. Breathe normally. Allow yourself to relax.

-Mastering the environment & perception/judgment-

Once you really practice this mediation, you will be able to do it on command, faster and easier. A relaxing mantra, picturing your calm place, deep breathing, pinching a pressure point, whatever your method – find one to insta-calm yourself into a peaceful place. In this way, we control all we can control, ourselves. Think about it like this, nature has given us examples of how to deal with chaos. Imagine that life is a hurricane, swirling danger all around us and, we are the eye in the storm. The ability to be at peace during chaos is important because, we do not function optimally when stressed. To diminish stress, visualize it outside of yourself swirling in that hurricane. Being calm lets us see clearer and allows us to better identify what to stress and what not to stress. Know this, you can only do what you can do, so have faith in yourself and your abilities, no stress and put all your energy to what you love cuz ain't that much time left, life is shorter than we can imagine. Be the eye in the storm.

-Mind over MATTER-

Put your mind over only what matters. Dick does this by focusing mental, physical and emotional energy on one thing. All our energy devoted to one goal at a time. This increases positivity thru results, decreases stress levels and allows us to feel progress in our lives. These are all inexorably linked. The mind creates positive energy which increases productivity. Stress is counterproductive and is a distraction to our focus of energy when it manifests into worry and doubt. We need to learn how to focus our energy because it does as we say. There are two ways to do so I say…

We can shine like a light bulb

Or

focus like a laser.

Basically, we can exude our energy in all directions, or focus and make a more forceful impact in one direction. We are all creators, we are here to create. We are all vibrating on different levels, in the same plane of existence. Our goal is to come together on this physical plane, to unify and consciously affect our own evolution. We are at a unique point in history, a fork in the road, a paradigm shift in our mental capabilities, our spiritual essence and our energy signature. But first before we unify our world, we must unify the most important part of our worlds, ourselves. WE are the missing link in our world that will bring our ideals into reality. It's up to us to be personally focused in our spirit, mind and body to promote the unity we need to reach as beings. Once we have united our self, only then can we be united with others. Life distracts us, splintering our interests and dividing our power. We must take it back and focus it in the direction we choose. We have to be strategic in how we use time in the present to improve time in the future. We have to delve deeply into ourselves, in how we see, value and employ TIME.

-Time is Greater than Money-

How many of us make money? How many of us save money? How many of us keep money? How many of us put our money to work? Money is an important part of life - not the most important part as we know but a close third. As its value is set by the economy to provide our needs & wants it can have variable worth. There are people who are rich and poor. There are people who look rich and are poor and who look poor and are rich. Perception is reality but we are the masters of our perception. Perception starts with what we think and feel about ourselves so as with any journey, it starts within. Focus your finances and aim your money in the direction you want to go in. Invest in yourself first, your dreams and your career. If you want to make a lot of money, do what you love. If you want to have a rich life, spend time with your family often, take in the moments with them and do things you love.

-the ART of communication-

Listen & express with consideration for yourself & the feelings of others. I try to treat others with the patience of a parent or a teacher. I think we are all students and teachers simultaneously. Consider who it is you are addressing, their communication style and figure how best to address them and their needs. Listen, learn the communication style of the speaker and respond accordingly. This will facilitate many of your relationships and conversations. But first, before we get to communicating with others, a break for a Self-ie! Rather, a moment to reflect on how you speak to yourself. The internal dialogue…

- <u>Internal Dialogue</u> – Be aware of how you treat yourself, even on the smallest level of internal communication – our internal dialogue. That's the voice inside our head. We each have one, we use it to think in our minds. How we speak here is a sign of how you will speak to and treat others. Speak lovingly to yourself and it will radiate into your world. Be mindful. Be at peace here in your mind. I liken the state of being the *eye in the storm of life* here as well; at peace, calm and confidently in control; A confidence that comes with acceptance of self.

- <u>Objectivity and decision-making</u>– see all sides of the argument and make the best decision that benefits the most people. Like playing POOL or

Billiards its important to see all the angles in any moment of deliberation. It's important to gather facts, consider contrary opinions and research truth, if you seek it. Once your due diligence is done, have some "COJONES". Simple and plain, grow some courage and take a manageable risk and a step toward your dream. Risk, no matter how low, is risk to accept nonetheless. Play within your means, take baby steps. Plan your work and work your plan – and when decision time comes, this is when you play your cards. You've done your research, calculated your risk and are prepared to make the decision. You must trust yourself and have the confidence to make the call. TRUST YOURSELF. Start by listening to yourself. We are all tapped into the pool of infinite knowledge and energy, we ask questions and we receive answers. At times were not listening enough or liking what we hear back enough to follow the advice. TRUST YOURSELF. We are unique creatures created divinely, fashioned in love and genius. We are the reason there is a missing link, we are the jump in evolution that puzzles scientists for a reason. We are in a constant state of self-discovery and rebirth. Every man and woman, at birth, is created equal. After that, it's on us to figure out. We are the weight on our scales, so get your weight up in balance to work the scales to tip in your favor. Once we're born, our parents and our decisions create momentum/energy into our lives. Where we go from there, is based on the choices we make and, in the Time is greater than Money philosophy, the choices that bring the most are spending time with those we love and helping others.

- <u>Relationship Mastery:</u> People are in our lives for a reason, a season or a lifetime. Be aware of who you are around, opening up as you would for a lifetime person when you're dealing with a reason or season person, could cause you unhappiness and to have unmet expectations. Making good judgment calls will help us to identify when we can represent for ourselves, get in touch with our inner dick. We can't make everyone happy, and it's not our responsibility to. Our intention should be to make ourselves happy. Be ourselves: express ourselves and let ourselves live and breathe. Since we can't control someone else, or their happiness, to invest energy into such an effort would be wasteful. We seek efficiency, to do the most with the least, whether it is time or energy, to walk the path of least resistance and accomplish our list of things to do. Our evolution is self-imposed.   We will it to be through choices we make, primarily with our understanding and, subsequent investment of, TIME.

- _Mastering the moment_ -

Life comes in all sizes, shapes and forms – big and small – but it's always bigger than we know and more than we can imagine. So, if we're somewhere in the middle of life, so should be our perspective of it. It's important to maintain an objective perspective on life, so as to not miss something by being too engaged by something else. For example, looking at an impressionist artwork or a paint by number picture and just looking at the reds – you would miss the picture by focusing on one aspect of the painting - so Life is about achieving a healthy balance - Enjoying life in moderation so you get the whole picture, by experiencing its myriad facets. Taking in the moments, like a breath of fresh air… Life is a bunch of moments we control depending on how we put them together. So the more in control of our schedule we are the more in control of our moments we are. Mastering the moment can lead to controlling the future, since our future is just a union of these moments to come. How we fill those moments, is fully in our control. Choose wisely.

Tip: Make a list for yourself, a bucket list maybe, of things you want to do before you die.   Things you have to do, feelings you have to experience, places you have to see. Check off 3 per year like clockwork. Plan your work, work your plan. The same way you would read a book, word by word, line by line, page by page write **and follow** your life plan.

WISDOM
lies in
WONDER
– Socrates

-Curiosity-

Stay curious about the world around you! Keep your inner child alive, wonder what secrets the world still holds for you to discover, there are always more...If I could recommend places for you to see to expand your perceptions of the world and life as we know it....they would be to visit the most ancient sites of the world, the ruins of other worlds, other ages on Earth. We have offered each other the unique opportunity to appreciate our divinity throughout History, and have left clues of our development for future generations to study. Respect your elders and learn from them. The more we learn from the past, the more we change our present and further evolve our future. Getting in touch with your Inner Dick leads to growing in knowledge and over-standing of life and our human history, in its entirety.

These are some of the thing that make me wonder...

- Washington DC from the Sky- Celestial alignments & Global architecture

- The Constitution, the Bill of Rights, the Capitol Building

Washington D.C. Monument – Pyramid with a spiral sstaircase

- The Grand Canyon (History in rock timeline)

- The Georgia Guide stones (U.S.A.)

- Egyptian Pyramids – Pyramid of Giza

- Sinai Peninsula

- Great Wall of China

- Temple of Heliopolis, Ba'albek, Lebanon

- Mexican Pyramids - Mexico City, Tenochtitlan, Xcaret, Chichen Itza

- Guatemalan/Honduran Pyramids

- Jewish, Iraqi and Antarctic Pyramids

- Macchu Picchu, Peru (city in the clouds)

- Bermuda Triangle (Caribbean) Atlantis

- The Ring of Fire (Pacific Ocean) Lemuria

- The Marianas Trench

- Sumerian Tablets

- Emerald Tablets of Thoth

-Physical Mastery-

- Covered in many other books, videos and boot camp classes. You should be healthy, physically and in control of your physical self, enough to reach complete Mastery. Controlling breath through meditation is where we focus here for physical mastery but Yoga is highly recommended as well.

Afterthought

The Beginning of you...

Life changes, even as we are living it changes in ways we could never imagine. Acceptance of our ultimate passing is important to us and our loved ones. My view is that it is a part of life that is inevitable and since it is as such, it has to be part of life. I can't believe we spend our lives developing to a level and then ending all that. We are too beautiful in spirit, too developed in mind to waste such a resource. Science teaches us the laws of physics state energy cannot be destroyed only changed; also that we are all energy, vibrating at different speeds...I guess this is where the Math comes in, 1 + 1 = 2. We will change, we will pass but we will remain somewhere in the Great Beyond. Begin in this moment what will build and last for all time, your indomitable spirit.

When it comes to Knowledge, know your history, know your rights. Know the laws and their nuances. For every action there is an equal and opposite reaction. Life has been evolving and playing out for thousands of years, we should respect it as such. Life itself is beautiful and priceless and we should treat it with the highest regard, we need to teach each other this truth. Time is worth more than money. The second part of knowledge is sharing it.

TIME IS GREATER THAN MONEY

TIME MONEY

VOLUME I

WRITTEN BY RAMÓN DE LA CRUZ

1. Friends

2. Merry

3. Peace

4. Jokes

5. Home Cooked Meals

6. A difference

7. Plans

8. Love

9. Your Masterpiece

10. Miracles

The question pondered most by great thinkers throughout History. What does it all mean? What is life about?

This one is simpler than we all think and deeper than we think at the same time. The meaning of life is to Live. That's it. Live your life how you feel right living it, in harmony with the world around you. We complicate it with choice but the actual answer is simple. How you choose to Live determines whether you're living it or, if it is living you. What you decide your life will be is what it will become. The object is to define yourself and leave your creative and positive mark on the world. Life is there for us to mold to our specifications: To be whatever we have the courage to make of it. Our powers of mind over matter have the influence to accomplish anything we can conceive and believe or, any vision we can create and maintain. Life is about making an impact on life, on the life of those around you. Everybody dies but not everybody Lives. Sometimes I think the dead walking described in Revelation is an analogy for the "rat race" we see in our business world today; Waking up going to a job that makes you feel dead to the world. It was put to me most succinctly once when a comparison was made between those working at jobs they hate with the zombies in a popular AMC show by calling them the "The *Working* Dead".

"L.T.D." – Live the dream, that's the only way it will ever be lived or realized by humanity. Live more than you can imagine, make modest goals, surprise yourself by exceeding them and build your own personal momentum in life.

LIVE it fully.

Ramon Flow:

This can't be life, can't really be the highest of the high

There's got to be much more than just to live and die

So my pick is to inspire, spark the mind, here's the fire,

Tres S. ya'll, Doing my best to be remembered

Here's a memoir,

A true artiste of this here craft,

Like a Renoir, Delta te presenta,

Some shit to switch perceptions like Katrina

If it goes over ya head, you got ya feet up

Freestyles spit once and never repeat 'em

Thank God for your cd kids, your breathin, your eatin

There's more to life than weekends, tv's and beatin

Time speeding, feeling the heat out in the evening;

This can't be life so I'll be on that last train dreamin.

I think it's safe to say, we can agree upon certain truths in Life. Truths like Love, Truth, Gravity/Karma and Energy can't be destroyed only changed...etc. I thought it would serve us best to read through some of these subconsciously agreed upon beliefs we have. Getting in touch with your Inner Dick in this instance is being the opposite of what the world shows. The world is a negative place, so Dick is positive in the face of the adversity of the negative world. It takes a Dick to be positive among pessimists. It takes inner strength to be persistent in the face of criticism and adversity.

Humans are like trees, we can take something and turn it into something better, like carbon to oxygen we can change negative to positive.

Just have faith in the power of your positivity

When in doubt, be a Scout.

Be a Boy Scout – trustworthy, loyal, helpful, friendly, courteous, kind, obedient, cheerful, thrifty, brave, clean and reverent.

Balance your life, Enjoy a little bit of all that life has to offer,

Formula for Creating Luck (Hard work + Opportunity=LUCK)

Do what you love. You aren't here to do anything else as well as that.

Live by the Universal truths

Stay true to your principles and morals

Do unto others. Do good deeds.

Be kind. Spread LOVE.

Be Reverent and humble.

Socialize.

Have faith in Humanity.

Have faith in Hu-manity.

ASK QUESTIONS!

Pay close attention to your leaders and elected officials.
Absolute power corrupts absolutely.

Leave room for nature…Leave room for nature.
Do what feels right.

We as humans have an innate sense of truth,
So trust your intuition,
Develop it along with intelligence.

Respect your divinity.

Karma is a universal law,
The law of action and its equal and opposite reaction –

We are all "board members" of
   The spiritual collective conscience,
     It is our responsibility to upload our experiences
through meditation, through connection with one another.

No matter where you go, there you are.

There is no escape from your destiny or,
what you were meant to do

However, your fate or, how it happens,
     can be influenced by your actions.
Over standing of what is happening around us is our key
to maximizing influence.

What we put out, will inexorably be returned to us,
the way water expelled from our planet in a past collision
returns to us in the form of shooting stars and comets in the sky.

Personality begins where Comparison ends.

What we put out into the world, what comes from our mind and is created into our physical world, is what we will get back. Therefore, being kind to one another could be the most selfish act we can perform, because we know as energy flows, it will flow back to us with better returns than Warren Buffet could forecast.

Say what you need to say, honestly and respectfully.

Don't take time for granted.

"Things may come to those who wait, but only the things left by those who hustle. - Abraham Lincoln

Lead by Example, talk is cheap

"Creativity is intelligence having fun."
— Albert Einstein

The Time is greater than Money philosophy speaks to living more aligned with naturally perfect laws in a world that tries to rewrite them.

Chapter 7: 1st Love (Denyin yourself)

In any relationship and especially in Marriages, gitwyid means maintaining your sexual tension and sense of mystery. Familiarity breeds contempt so keeping a comfortable distance, even from people we love dearly, is healthy. I think this is what couples mean when they refer to the "spark" being gone. So be a little bit of a dick and keep some playful space and mystery between you and the one you love, to maintain that "spark." Make time for each other but take time for yourself as well.

At work, gitwyid takes on a more supportive role. This is the exception to the rule. In this case, we need to learn to be more fluid, flexible and complementary when we are in positions of Leadership and Influence.

A boss works with fear,

A leader crafts confidence.

A boss seeks to blame,

A leader sees opportunity in challenges.

A boss thinks they know everything,

A leader leans on actual experts.

A boss makes work boring,

A leader makes it fun and exciting.

A boss is interested in themselves only,

A leader considers and cares for others.

~ A word to all the people who claim they leaders or "the BOSS".

-anonymous

Getting in touch with your inner dick in this instance is not about being a "Dick" (Dick, a colloquial vulgarism for the penis. *Also used to describe an inconsiderate person) abusive, taking advantage of others or in any manner being pretentious, inappropriate or offensive. The point of getting in touch with your inner dick is to tap into your inner strength to stand your ground when necessary. This is especially important in positions of power, when you come up against many different opinions. GITWYID for employers and managers means leading beyond the normal work aspect of things, delving into the very human nature of management. A manager or employer is a leader, setting the tone, atmosphere and productivity of their workplace and employees. If you want your employees to think out of the box for you and be productive, think out of the box for them. People in power are leaders, whether they want to be or not and, usually, happily accept the responsibility. Leaders set the environment up everywhere; as Government does for society, as parents or caregivers do at home and as coaches & players on a team or in the boardroom do. They set the tone, therefore any tone they feel uncomfortable with, they are charged with leading into positive growth. Leadership transcends boundaries, which is a key to identifying when something is worthwhile because anything that transcends boundaries brings people together. I think Getting in touch with your Inner Dick transcends boundaries and speaks to us all, putting race, sex, and finances to the side to focus on the part that gives all those factors life, People.*

This is a philosophy intended to inspire leaders to take charge of their positions and keep looking for innovative ways to motivate, teach and grow both their internal and external business relationships. We are all leaders somewhere so this applies to everyone. Whether we provide positive or negative leadership, our influence will be felt around us. The question is what kind of impact do you want to have and where? Your influence is built from your relationships, from the respect of your peers and society's perspective of you. Your influence runs parallel with your reputation. As a person in power, we are familiar with defending from attacks on our reputations. Defense should always be handled diplomatically and honestly. Grace under fire/duress is something that grows the reputation and your influence. Experience shows that we are better served in the long run by handling things calmly. It shows the other parties involved that you are a person who can get things done through adversities. Being patient and respectful of others is the key to building relationships. A key to being patient is having an understanding that we are all on our own paths, developing in the time that is right for us. We each need to be able to recognize this, and spur each others development. Build your network to build your net worth. Getting in touch with your inner dick can help you gain power by improving your relationships. Achieving Mastery of this power comes when we learn the ebb and flow of the tides of life; the nuances of life and interpersonal dynamics of energy involved in our existence. Dick's philosophy here is that life is like surfing in that you have to know when to go against the tide and when to ride with the wave (though I have never successfully surfed, I've always admired the prowess of balance and control needed to do it). The subtleties of life are most interestingly met with meted power. "You get more with honey than vinegar." Those in power are responsible for Leadership, Mentoring and Teaching; Delegation and Independence. This is the recipe for growing your circle of influence; improve the quality of the relationships already within them. "Be like Mike" Michael Jordan improved the teammates around him and we too have the ability to do this, once we find our basketball...Once you have power, GITWYID means using it wisely. In a world where temptation is everywhere, this is the hard thing to do.

Chapter 8: Faith and Karma

One thing Religions agree on is that there is something greater than us. Faith means truly believing and trusting in that other dimensional, greater and omnipotent power. Getting in touch with your Inner Dick means knowing when to trust and when to toil but always have faith in your abilities. I believe we should be students of the World and learn all Religions. My theory is they each hold a certain perspective of the truth and keeping an open mind is essential to learning the whole truth. Science calls these things the laws of physics but, beyond them lays even greater mysteries like intelligent life, the Human Divinity code, and Karma. I think Karma is Gravity in form we don't yet understand. After all no matter how far we shoot something out into space, most times, it will come back. There's no gravity in space but, there must be. How else do planets hold their satellites and moons in orbit but through their gravitational pull? It's what holds us on the ground of this beautiful planet of ours called Earth. The same force that applies to our physical body and energy, applies to our mental and emotional energies.

In this aspect of life, GITWYID means keeping an open mind in a world that is constantly trying to distract and reprogram you, focusing consciously on doing the right thing, putting out positive energy and knowing to have faith in your abilities. Have faith in whoever/whatever you believe in; that you believe in anything good is what's important in the big picture. Learn about the good in all religions and beliefs; be open to the different ways we are all telling the same story. Faith and truth are like puzzles; we need to get all the pieces to truly see the BIG picture. Remember to believe in something greater because, there is always something greater. I believe in LOVE. Remember to be humble and to allow yourself to be humbled by the beauty around you.

Ramón De La Cruz

LOVE

THE ALBUM

A 3DLCE.COM PRODUCTION

PARENTAL ADVISORY EXPLICIT CONTENT

So, Time is greater than money volume 1 is almost done. Maybe you're in touch with your Inner Dick or already were and treat your time like the most precious resource you have. If so, Congratulations! You are part of an elite club of readers who were brave enough to read my musings and make it through them psychologically unscathed, hopefully ☺. A club that includes those who've learned how to retune themselves into life's nuances and coincidences; that it's ok to go with a take no shit attitude and to go with the flow depending on the situation; That if YOU are not you, no one else will ever be...

So now what?

It doesn't stop here. As we evolve so does how we exert ourselves, our influence and, our (inner dick) energy. Humans tend to stray while enjoying the comforts of good times into complacency. This is what we must guard against now that we are in touch with ourselves, feel the synchronicity of life and the right decisions becoming easier to come by. We have to maintain our open mind by continuously learning new things, operating out of our comfort ones and re-educating ourselves. Now that you are in the flow, you must maintain the flow. GITWYID in this Chapter symbolizes your rebirth and rededication to living your life to the fullest. What could be more important than feeling great about your life because you are doing things you have always wanted to do? You started out too scared, or shy, or nervous. Be brave now: Be bold. You are in ever changing times, be a pioneer. Dream new things and bring them to life. Live your life to your standards and always be open to new lessons and opportunities. Love yourself and Love others that deserve it completely. Maintain yourself by treating yourself well, eating healthy, exercising and meditating. Keep your dreams and goals in focus and most of all, always remember that your evolution is never over, it continues into death as our energies evolve into different state of being. Prepare for life after you and get rid of your fear of death, learn to embrace it and see it as the natural part of life that it is. Use this thought whenever your mind strays into complacency to strike it back to its needed sense of urgency. You are ultimately responsible for yourself and your evolution and, above all, relish this personal freedom through knowing this and trust yourself. Calm your mind to focus its power. Love yourself enough to do so. GITWYID means making the time for your SELF as easily as you would for a holiday, party or your kid's basketball game.

GITWYID➔SITWYID
Get in touch with your ID➔Stay in touch with your ID

Don't be afraid to be yourself, to make choices and live with the lessons, don't be afraid to make a few mistakes now and then, and don't be afraid to dream of things no one has dreamed before. Trust yourself; humans are innately blessed with intuitive powers. We seek a connection, to what we don't know. All we know is a constant ringing in our intuition, mocking us, reminding us of a time when we were connected. So let me welcome you to the obvious. That is now. You are connected to the infinite energy, memory and synergy of the universe. You are as you choose to be; as you make yourself to be in the now. As individuals we can spread this knowledge and replicate our metamorphosis from the ground up. But, can we truly reach the critical mass necessary to evolve to the next level? I think we already have.

Scientists measure and study society's "feelings or trends" using data compiled into graphs called algorithms. I theorize that we are all one, born of the same elements as stars and have a shared consciousness, so, why wouldn't that include emotion?

Women who spend time together tend to sync their monthly cycles. Parents and their children sometimes develop an uncanny 6th sense, Lovers often say they experience this as well. So, a connection is established. It's imperative for us to maintain our own happiness for this reason exactly. All emotion can snowball, it's up to us to control and direct it or else it can affect the people and atmosphere around us. Peace is found within, there is none without. Emotional Mastery for the Human Race can be achieved by each of us reaching individually to the common goal. We'll get there. I am a firm believer in our untapped potential. A potential with programmed genetic directives that allow for free will to exert its influence over reality. We can move mountains if we want.

We each have our purpose here whether we choose to pursue it or not. There is an energy among us that directs us; we can choose to ignore or follow it. The destination is always the same. We can choose to be part of it, go with our gut and see it through or, go away from it. But, we can not run from our destinies or their destinations. They are our life's orbit; our souls gravitational pull.

Everything happens for a reason.

We should note that, even though we may not see or understand why, we have to believe that we can make things better no matter what happens or why it happens. We ARE the good we seek. The positive pioneers of our time. Yet, we're humble enough to know that we don't know everything. If we did, our technology would have positive side effects like the natural technology that existed here before us. Sometimes what seems bad actually is good in the long run and vice-versa.

And if not, chalk it up to your mistake, forgive yourself and move on. Lesson learned. But let the lesson open you up to the next experience. Live your life freely, with the understanding gained giving you confidence to see through your endeavors through every obstacle."

   - Controlling the future by managing now:
   Mastery of Self/moment/future
   - Strength – (inner and physical/spiritual/mental/emotional)
   - Take care of yourself/body/spirit/mind, caring for your temple
   - SHINE like a light bulb or FOCUS like a laser.
   - You must give to get, you must sacrifice to get your wish.
   - Follow the Golden Rule "Do unto others…"

- Know your self – your history, your goals and future-vision

- Know your history, your world, your planet.

- You are what you eat, physically, mentally, emotionally

-(birds of a feather) like energies attract

- Teach children, whenever you can. Mentor someone and Share the knowledge

- ID what you love to do and Just Do It.

- Develop your senses, as many as you can, they are infinite as the dimensions of existence. Specifically, judgment, danger sensing (situational awareness), first 5 senses, mental senses, instant ESP

- Develop your mind, memory capacity

- Be a leader, an innovator, not a follower, not a consumer, a producer, a creator, set standards. We are in tune with our spiritual frequencies when creating.

- STRIVE TO BE THE BEST, TO PERFECT YOUR CRAFT

- Understand the scheme of things and where you fit in

- Learn to understand and Respect your feelings, organize your thoughts, and Express yourself (It's about presentation)

Leave life better than you left it. Boy Scouts rule #1, leave nature cleaner than where you found it. Apply it to life as whole, and be the improvement you envision in life. Embody your ideal. This is a pure human purpose, altruism. Good for the good of all.

If you ever try to surf or windsurf, you know that it is about achieving a balance. A balance between push and pull, wind and wave, self and surf. You push against the current to ride it back to shore. You know when to go against the flow and when to ride it back effortlessly. In life, we find a similar balance. Sometimes you're paddling out and waiting for the right time: Sometimes you ride the waves. It comes down to time and effort and those moments become memory. Slow down to see the moments. As the world and life whips around us, remember nature's lesson in the hurricane, there is an eye of the storm; A place of peace and calm within the storm, peace within chaos. Thus, more than one truth can exist because truth is perspective, it is relative to the person with the belief. So remember your Monet Moment principle, to balance yourself and your perspective. Once you can see the moment, being in the moment enables you to influence the moment. Practice the patience to let moments develop. Take the time to make moments develop, small things build over time. Seeds become forests, practice becomes perfected; Time becomes a life. Learn to play chess, or any game that is strategic. It helps to develop your mind and intuition. Knowing WHEN to do WHAT is critical because timing is everything. Doing the same thing over is necessary, as repetitive practice is required to improve anything. Make slight changes and set small goals you can achieve each day. Master the moment. Then put that on repeat. Automating the simpler parts of your life help free the spirit by escaping the mundane to experience the something greater. Develop your judgment by learning from these slight changes and it will engage your ability to intuitively know what's right for you. Develop your trust in self so when things get difficult you can help yourself keep going through them. Never give up. Master your moment.

We often miss the repeating simplicity of moments, or, the chance to take what we've learned and apply it to a new situation. The simplicity of moments, or, the fact that life is created of an eternity of these moments, allows us to break down life, and through mastery of the moment, master the future and our lives. Make each moment matter, treat everything with the energy of your first day, your first project, your life dream, because that's your life's purpose, to fulfill that dream and improve the spiritual conditions we are in. We are each a step in the evolution of humanity. Scary sometimes, isn't it…How important each of us actually is to the whole? …Scary but, beautifully liberating as well.

In that light we find purpose; in that unknown lies what we seek.

We all want to be part of something... Then realize that we all are already part of something, something larger than we can imagine: History. What story will be told of you? What legacy will you leave? How will it compare to those before us and those to come? I see the future as bright; I'm hopeful good will win out. At least we know we have the potential to make it so. Stay in touch with your Inner Dick.

It's a new day, a new you; a brave new world. Only difference is, you're brave enough now to face it head on. Be confident with yourself, be brave, have some co-jones, make mistakes once and learn from them, speed up the evolution of man by being better at living. When we get out of our own way, life has a funny way of meeting us halfway. Life delivers if you're home to sign for the package. I am not saying to wait at home for something to happen. I am saying if you are in it 100%, Life will respond to your effort. Follow your vision. Follow your heart, even when the people who love you can't see it yet. The important thing to share is the results, not the mission. Stay Strong, Stay focused and let nothing stand in the way of your goals. Whatever you do ripples across the expanse of energy we all share. You'll get where you want to go by going. See YOU there...

TIME IS GREATER THAN MONEY

VOLUME I

To be or not to be...in this moment. Calm.
The eye of the storm courtesy of Mother Nature's blueprint.
If your eyes can feel and your heart can see then you too will agree that Time is greater than Money.
Time can't be remade, is often traded below market value and is the first resource we all have to work with.
Time is the great equalizer. Once we are gone, Money and material, if wisely invested, can outlast us.
Yet even with that, isn't the essence of memory rooted in the time you spent in life and not the money?
Your worth is what YOU make it and it is based off of the investment of your time and your interest.
So about that moment...what's it worth to you? What are you worth to you?

- Coming soon for FREE download at 3DLCE.com-

Time Is Greater Than Money Volume 2 : The Poems to LOVE

"LOVE! The Album"
coming to all stores and streaming services soon!

9 781737 197409